African-American Soldiers

Black Fighting Men: A Proud History

Catherine Reef

Twenty-First Century Books

A Division of Henry Holt and Company New York

Twenty-First Century Books
A Division of Henry Holt and Company, Inc.
115 West 18th Street
New York, NY 10011

Henry Holt® and colophon are trademarks of
Henry Holt and Company, Inc.
Publishers since 1866

Text Copyright © 1994 by Catherine Reef
All rights reserved.
Published in Canada by Fitzhenry & Whiteside Ltd.,
195 Allstate Parkway
Markham, Ontario L3R 2T8

Library of Congress Cataloging-in-Publication Data

Reef, Catherine
Black fighting men: a proud history / Catherine Reef. — 1st ed.
p. cm. — (African-American soldiers)
Includes bibliographical references and index.
1. United States—Armed forces—Afro-Americans—Juvenile literature. 2.
United States—Armed Forces—Biography—Juvenile literature. 3. United
States—History, Military—Juvenile literature. [1. United States—Armed
Forces—Afro-Americans. 2. United States—History, Military. 3. Soldiers.
4. Afro-Americans—Biography.]
I. Title. II. Series.
U52.R44 1994
355'.0092'273—dc20   93-44279 CIP AP

ISBN 0-8050-3106-5
First edition—1994

Printed in Mexico
All first editions are printed on acid-free paper ∞.

10 9 8 7 6 5 4 3 2 1

Contents

Introduction

American history is a story of people building a country—people from many backgrounds creating a government, settling in towns and cities, and starting traditions. It is the story of Americans defending their nation in times of war.

The Africans who traveled to American shores before the Civil War came against their will. They came as slaves and so were denied the rights and choices that white settlers enjoyed. Even when the slaves gained their freedom, America treated them unfairly.

But despite prejudice and unfair treatment, African Americans have been strong defenders of the United States. They have fought with courage and patriotism in every American war, from the war for independence through the war in the Persian Gulf. Again and again, they have proven themselves equal to whites.

Today women are starting to take on a larger role in the armed forces. Until recently, however, the story of blacks in the military was a story of men—men who won victories against America's enemies and against racism.

Some black fighting men have become well-known public figures. Many Americans, for example, recognize General Colin Powell. As the first black chairman of the Joint Chiefs of Staff, Powell held the nation's highest military job.

Most people who make history, though, are far less prominent. All of the heroes described in this book were ordinary people doing extraordinary things.

Chapter 1

The Revolutionary War

Crispus Attucks

In September 1750, Deacon William Brown of Framingham, Massachusetts, placed an ad in the *Boston Gazette*. Brown offered a reward for the return of a runaway slave, a man six feet, two inches tall, having "short curl'd Hair" and "Knees nearer together than common." The escaped slave was Crispus Attucks, the first person to die in the American struggle for independence.

Crispus Attucks was born in Framingham in the early 1720s, at a time when whites in all of England's thirteen American colonies were allowed to own black slaves.

Following his escape, Attucks sought freedom by going to sea. But English laws and taxes made it hard for anyone to feel free in colonial America. England's Navigation Acts forced shippers to transport their cargoes to British ports.

The laws controlled the prices that England would pay for those goods. The colonists paid taxes on paper, glass, and other imported items—taxes they considered high and unfair.

With every new tax or law, the colonists grew more defiant. Some talked about fighting for their independence. England sent a force of red-coated soldiers to the city of Boston in 1768, hoping to keep the peace. But to the people of Boston, the military men were bright red symbols of English tyranny. The colonists confronted the soldiers with angry words, and fights broke out. Among redcoats and citizens, nerves were on edge. People had been wounded; how long would it be until someone was killed?

Crispus Attucks was working on the Boston waterfront on the cold evening of March 5, 1770, when word reached the docks that a British sentry had injured a boy. Many felt that the time had come to act. And when a crowd moved through the city streets, Crispus Attucks led the way. Strong and stout, Attucks's "very looks were enough to frighten any person," said John Adams, who would become the second president of the United States.

The mob, armed with clubs and rocks, vowed to drive the British troops from Boston. "They have no business here!" the colonists cried. Soon the colonists stood face to face with a group of soldiers and their commanding officer, Captain Thomas Preston. The townspeople dared the soldiers to shoot. But the men in uniform had been forbidden to fire their weapons without a direct order from the civil magistrate, the English official charged with keeping order.

A group of colonists, Crispus Attucks among them, raised their clubs and struck at the soldiers' muskets. They accused Preston's force of lacking the courage to fire. "Be not afraid," Attucks called confidently to the mob. "They dare not shoot."

But the taunts and blows proved too much for the soldiers to withstand. At last, without orders, one raised his gun and shot Crispus Attucks in the chest. The freedom-loving seaman fell dead. More gunfire quickly followed, and four more colonists lost their lives. "On that night, the foundation of American independence was laid," commented John Adams. America would remember the skirmish of March 1770 as the Boston Massacre.

Thousands attended the funeral for the shooting victims. The people of Boston buried the five in a common tomb. In the years that followed, the Americans fought for independence in the Revolutionary War. Five thousand African Americans joined the war effort. Black soldiers took part in the early fighting at Concord, Massachusetts, in

The Crispus Attucks Monument

CRISPUS ATTUCKS
SAMUEL MAVERICK
JAMES CALDWELL
SAMUEL GRAY
PATRICK CARR

MARCH 5. 1770.

1775. They helped to win other important battles, such as the Battle of Bunker Hill, fought outside Boston, and the two battles that took place in Saratoga, New York, in 1777. Throughout the war, which ended in 1781, Crispus Attucks was a symbol of courage and sacrifice to the cause of liberty.

George Washington, commander of the Continental Army and first president of the United States, used flowery language to sum up Attucks's contribution. "When the Colonists were staggering wearily under the cross of woe," said Washington, "a Negro came to the front and bore the cross to the victory of glorious martyrdom."

In 1888, the people of Boston dedicated a monument to Crispus Attucks and the other colonists who died in the Boston Massacre. Today, visitors to Boston can stand at the site of the massacre, marked by a circle of cobblestones where State and Congress streets intersect.

Chapter 2
The War of 1812

Jordan B. Noble

"As sons of freedom you are now called upon to defend our most inestimable blessing." Bony, scarfaced Andrew Jackson spoke to an audience of free black men. Calling them "fellow citizens," the white general urged the African Americans to join his fighting force.

It was December 1814. The United States had been at war with England for more than two years. The Americans fought this conflict, remembered as the War of 1812, for the right to sail safely on the ocean. England had been seizing American ships and "impressing" seamen. The British took the American sailors into custody and forced them to fight in England's war against France.

The War of 1812 was fought largely on the seas. The United States had won naval victories on the Atlantic, the Great Lakes, and Lake

Champlain. Then in September 1814, the British marched into Washington, D.C., and set fire to the White House and the Capitol. Now Jackson had come to Louisiana to prevent the British from capturing New Orleans. He appealed to the black population for help.

Hundreds of African Americans answered Jackson's call, among them a thirteen-year-old boy named Jordan Noble. Jackson promised them the same compensation that white soldiers received: $124 and 160 acres of land. He also promised them glory. "You will, undivided, receive the applause and gratitude of your countrymen," he said.

The clashes known as the Battle of New Orleans began on a foggy night, two days before Christmas. Jackson received word that the British had taken possession of a Louisiana sugar plantation. The British planned to eat a hot meal and get a good night's rest before moving on to New Orleans. "By the Eternal," Jackson vowed, "they shall not sleep on our soil!"

Cautiously, Jackson's army moved toward the British encampment. Jordan Noble carried a drum instead of a weapon. As the unit's drummer boy, he did his part to defend his "most inestimable blessing"—his freedom.

All through the night march, 1,800 soldiers— black, white, and Native American—relied on

Noble's drumbeat to keep them together. The tap-tap-tap of Noble's drum guided them to the plantation, where they launched a surprise attack and dealt a serious blow to the British force. Jackson singled out his black soldiers for praise, telling them, "You surpass my hopes."

Black soldiers and sailors helped to win many battles of the War of 1812. One-sixth of all navy gunmen were free black men. Well-practiced experts, they handled the large guns on warships.

A wood engraving shows African-American riflemen during the Battle of New Orleans

General William Hull commended the black seamen on the U.S.S. *Constitution*, a famous American fighting vessel, after the crew destroyed a British warship. "I never had any better fighters," Hull said. "They stripped to the waist and fought like devils." The African Americans appeared "utterly insensible to danger and possessed with a determination to outfight white sailors," Hull noted.

The war ended in 1815, when the United States agreed to a treaty with England. The treaty failed to guarantee the seagoing rights for which the Americans had fought. But England's war with France was over. The Royal Navy no longer had a reason to impress American sailors.

Jordan Noble continued to serve the nation. It is believed that he went to Florida with Andrew Jackson to take part in the Seminole Wars. In the first half of the twentieth century, U.S. forces battled the Seminole Indians for possession of their land.

Military records show that Noble held the position of principal musician, First Regiment, Louisiana Volunteers, during the Mexican War. At the end of this war, fought between 1846 and 1848, the United States and Mexico agreed to consider the Rio Grande as the southern border of Texas. The United States acquired New Mexico and California from the Mexicans.

Very few African Americans served in the Mexican War. Although black soldiers had shown courage and patriotism in both the Revolution and the War of 1812, the army stopped enlisting black soldiers in 1820. "No Negro," an official army order plainly stated, "will be received as a recruit of the army."

Jordan Noble made his home in New Orleans between wars and became a well-known member of the free black community. In 1860, he received a medal in a ceremony at a New Orleans hotel. The United States honored Noble for his military service, although no African American had been enlisted as a soldier for forty years.

Chapter 3
The Civil War

Robert Smalls

Boats and the ocean were part of Robert Smalls's world from the time of his birth, in 1839. Growing up along the South Carolina coast, Robert and his brother, John, watched their father, a white man, cut and stitch canvas sails for ships. The boys' father could climb a ship's mast with ease to attach the heavy cloth to its rigging. He knew how to sail boats, too, and taught his sons about the geography of the coastline and the swift currents that move offshore.

Because his mother was a slave, Robert Smalls grew up in slavery. His owners made use of his maritime knowledge, putting him to work as a seaman when he became a young man. Soon Robert married and started a family.

Owning slaves had become illegal in the northern states in the early 1800s, but the practice continued in the South. The question of whether slavery was right or wrong caused anger and bitterness between Northerners and Southerners.

In April 1861, cannonballs sailed over the harbor of Charleston, South Carolina, as Southern guns fired on Fort Sumter, a U.S. Army post. Eleven Southern states had formed a separate nation, the Confederate States of America. They insisted that this was their right, just as it was their right to allow slavery. The gunfire in Charleston announced their determination to fight for that right. And it marked the start of the Civil War.

White men of the South marched off to fight in the Confederate army. Slaves were pressed into service, too, building roads and fortifications and growing food for the army. Robert Smalls was forced to pilot a transport ship, the *Planter*, which carried food and supplies to the Rebel forces.

Many slaves escaped to the Union, or Northern, side as soon as they could, and Robert Smalls was no exception. His opportunity came on May 12, 1862, when the *Planter*'s white officers spent the night in Charleston. Protected by darkness, Robert and John Smalls sneaked their families aboard ship. Then, in the early hours of May 13, Robert sailed out of Charleston's harbor and headed north. He delivered his passengers to freedom and presented the *Planter*—with its valuable cargo of munitions and food—to the Union forces.

The Northerners hired Robert Smalls to pilot the *Planter* for their side. At times the old cotton boat and its crew returned to Southern waters and came under Confederate attack. The shelling became so heavy along one South Carolina river that Smalls's white commanding officer ordered him to surrender the *Planter*. Smalls refused to do this, however. He knew that if they fell into the hands of the Confederates, his black crewmen would be killed or sold back into slavery. Smalls chose to fight. "Never, no, never, will I beach this boat," he said.

The frightened commander sought safety inside the steel bunker that held the *Planter*'s supply of coal. Robert Smalls stayed at his post. Although his boat was struck several times, he kept his head and steered out of danger. He then ordered a crew member to lock the cowardly officer in the coal bunker!

Smalls received praise for his courage, but some white naval officers resented his success. They arranged for the African-American pilot to make a difficult voyage, from Hilton Head, South Carolina, to Philadelphia, Pennsylvania. Smalls was sure to have trouble in the rough waters around Cape Hatteras, North Carolina, they told themselves. He would never get his boat through the Chesapeake Bay. The officers waited for Robert Smalls to fail.

But it was the officers who were outsmarted.

Before he left on his trip, Smalls spent three weeks studying maps of the Atlantic coastline. Although he had never learned to read, he made a chart of the coastal waters. He devised his own set of symbols for labeling the chart. Robert Smalls sailed smoothly into Philadelphia, where he began to educate himself in reading, writing, and mathematics.

On April 7, 1863, Smalls was back in Southern waters. He was piloting the *Keokuk*, an ironclad warship, in an attack on Charleston. The *Keokuk* was one of nine Union gunboats that attempted to travel the seven miles from the harbor entrance to the city. It was a treacherous trip. The ships had to move past large guns mounted at the mouth of the harbor. The Confederates had placed rope obstructions in the water, along with hidden explosives that would be detonated from shore when the ships passed over them.

The Southern guns battered the Union fleet. The *Keokuk* was struck ninety-nine times. But Robert Smalls sailed steadily forward. He was forced to abandon ship when his vessel finally sank.

The Battle of *Keokuk* ended in a Union loss. Navy leaders realized they could never capture Charleston by sea. The North would not take control of this Southern port until February 1865, following a nineteen-month siege. The South would surrender two months later.

An engraving of Robert Smalls

When the war was over, Smalls returned to South Carolina to live as a free man and begin a new career in government. He served in the state legislature and state senate, and in 1876 he was elected to Congress for the first of four terms. He worked to pass laws that would improve life for the former slaves.

Robert Smalls lived in Beaufort, South Carolina, after his retirement from public life. He died in 1915.

William Carney

The start of the Civil War brought hope to African Americans in the North and South—hope that a Union victory would mean the end of slavery. Throughout the North, African Americans tried to enlist in the armed forces, only to be turned away. Their white neighbors doubted the blacks' courage and fighting skill. White America planned to win the war on its own.

But after a year of fighting, the United States asked its black population for help. There were not enough white men to fill new regiments or replace the many soldiers who had been wounded or killed. The army formed a few units of black soldiers in 1862. In 1863, the government started enlisting blacks in earnest. By the war's end, 186,000 black soldiers would fight for the Union, and 38,000 would die.

William Carney was twenty-three years old when he joined the army in February 1863. His regiment, the 54th Massachusetts Colored Infantry, would be one of the most famous units—black or white—to fight in the Civil War.

William Carney was born to a slave mother and a free black father in Norfolk, Virginia, in 1840. Most blacks in the South had little opportunity for education, so William felt lucky to attend a secret school that was run by a minister. He learned to read and write under the preacher's guidance, and he developed a deep religious faith. "In my fifteenth year, I embraced the gospel," Carney wrote. He decided that one day he, too, would become a man of God.

Sometime during his teen years, William left Virginia and traveled to the whaling town of New Bedford, Massachusetts, hoping to work as a seaman. He earned money doing odd jobs and looked ahead to his career in the ministry. Then the Civil War began, and Carney postponed his plans.

William Carney joined an army that was strictly segregated. Black soldiers served in separate units from whites, and they took orders from white officers. Army leaders, still doubting that African Americans could fight, refused to let them command troops. The 54th Infantry and other black troops had to prove to the nation that they were just as brave and patriotic as whites.

Carney's regiment demonstrated its valor on July 18, 1863, as it led the Union charge on Fort Wagner, a Confederate stronghold. Built of sand and sticks on a thin strip of an island, Fort Wagner guarded the entrance to Charleston's harbor. The assault on Fort Wagner was part of the long Union siege to gain control of that city.

With the evening sky growing dim, the men

of the 54th moved toward Fort Wagner. They followed their color sergeant, the soldier who carried the regiment's flag into battle. All too soon, Carney saw the color sergeant go down. He hurried to the front of the attack and took the flag from the fallen man. Sergeant Carney held the flag high and led the way to the parapet, the thick wall surrounding the fort. He planted the flag at the top of the wall to give his regiment courage and guidance.

The 54th Infantry showed unusual bravery in the assault. Carney saw many of the men fall, wounded or dead. When the order came to retreat, he held the flag high again. Twice bullets struck him, and then a third one grazed his head. A soldier from New York, a man from another regiment, helped Carney retreat. He offered to carry the large, heavy flag, but Carney refused the man's aid. "No one but a member of the 54th should carry the colors," he explained.

The Confederates successfully defended Fort Wagner, but the 54th Infantry scored a victory for black America. They showed the nation that African Americans were the equal of white soldiers on the battlefield. They proved that, given the chance, blacks could be heroes.

William Carney became the first African American to earn the Medal of Honor, his country's highest military decoration. Estimates of the number of black Medal of Honor winners from the Civil War range between seventeen and twenty-six. Although Carney's wounds healed, they left him disabled. He was discharged from the army in June 1864.

Carney traveled to California to rebuild his strength in the warmth and sunshine. Then he settled in New Bedford with his wife and daughter. William Carney never became a minister. Instead, he delivered the mail in his community for thirty-two years.

As a well-known Civil War veteran, Carney was a popular speaker at Memorial Day services. The people of Boston asked him to take part in the ceremony when they dedicated a monument to the 54th Infantry in 1897.

Carney retired from the post office in 1901 and went to work at the State House, the building that housed the Massachusetts state government, in Boston. He enjoyed speaking to the schoolchildren who visited the State House and showing them the flag he carried during the assault on Fort Wagner. The famous flag had been displayed at the State House since the end of the Civil War.

On November 23, 1908, William Carney was injured in an elevator accident. When he died sixteen days later, the governor of Massachusetts ordered the flag at the State House flown at half mast. The state of Massachusetts, and the nation, had lost a hero.

Chapter 4

The Indian Wars/ The Spanish- American War

Augustus Wally

On August 16, 1881, Private Augustus Wally and the other soldiers of Company I, 9th Cavalry, were camped near the Cuchillo Negro Mountains of New Mexico. A rancher rushed into the camp, calling for help. A band of Indians had murdered his wife and children, he said. The soldiers of the 9th Cavalry rode out on their horses to aid the stricken man.

The 9th Cavalry was one of four regiments called Buffalo Soldiers, African Americans who served on the western frontier. The army formed these regiments—the 9th and 10th Cavalry and the 24th and 25th Infantry—following the Civil War. For the first time, black soldiers were allowed to serve when the country was at peace.

The frontier seemed far from peaceful, though. Settlers moving westward clashed repeatedly with the Native American tribes. The settlers wanted to farm and build towns on the Indians' land. They murdered many Indians and forced others onto patches of land called reservations. The native people fought hard to retain their land and freedom, and often killed in return. It was a tragic time in American history, a series of battles known as the Indian Wars.

The Buffalo Soldiers tried to keep peace, so the West could be settled without bloodshed. At times this task became impossible. Then their mission was to protect the settlers, citizens of their nation. They spent weeks and months tracking down bands of Indians who were committed to killing settlers and destroying their property.

Commanded by a white officer, Lieutenant George Burnett, Wally's company rode with the rancher to his home. They picked up the trail of the Native Americans, a trail leading into the mountains. The soldiers were after Nana, a chief of the Apache people. Strong, clever, and more than seventy years old, Nana wanted revenge. U.S. forces had killed many of his people and driven the others from their homeland.

Nana's warriors knew the mountain terrain well. By the time the Buffalo Soldiers caught up with them, they had taken cover behind rocks and in crevices. They were ready to fire their rifles at anyone who came near.

The soldiers tried to flank the Indians—to approach them from the right and left. The strategy failed, and the soldiers found themselves nearly surrounded. Lieutenant Burnett ordered a retreat. All of the soldiers moved back except for four men who did not hear the order. The Apaches moved in on those men, hoping to cut them off from the rest of the group.

The four trapped soldiers owed their lives to the bravery and quick thinking of Augustus Wally, who ran to their rescue. Two of the men had been wounded and could not move. Lieutenant Burnett and Wally picked them up and carried them to safety. Another Buffalo Soldier, Sergeant Moses Williams, held off the Apaches until Wally, Burnett, and the four soldiers retreated.

Nana would continue to fight against the U.S. forces until March 1885, when he surrendered to the army. He was one of seventy-seven Apaches who were loaded onto a freight train and sent to Fort Marion, Florida, to end their days as prisoners of war, far from the southwestern mountains they loved.

Augustus Wally received the Medal of Honor for his actions in the Cuchillo Negro Mountains. In all, seventeen black cavalrymen earned the nation's highest military honor in the Indian Wars.

Wally showed unusual courage in the West and then in Cuba, during the Spanish-American War.

The United States went to war with Spain in 1898, to help the island of Cuba gain its independence. American newspapers reported that the Cuban people received cruel treatment at the hands of their Spanish rulers. When an American battleship, the U.S.S. *Maine*, exploded in Havana Harbor, Cuba, Congress declared that a state of war existed between the United States and Spain.

Among the soldiers who traveled to Cuba were the four regiments of Buffalo Soldiers. Augustus

A Buffalo Soldier in the West is portrayed in this detail from "Scout's Out," a painting by Lee W. Brubaker

29

Wally and the others became the first African Americans to fight in a foreign land. They distinguished themselves in several key battles, helping to win the short war.

One of those battles took place at Las Guasimas, a gap in the jungle-covered hills. Wally was firing his rifle, hiding behind a bush for cover, when some motion caught his eye. Major B. F. Bell, a white officer, had been shot in the leg. Another officer, Captain G. Ayers, was struggling to move him to safety. Augustus Wally quickly saw that Ayers could not move the wounded man alone. He left the security of his hiding place and ran toward the two men.

Spanish marksmen shooting from a trench made the rescue especially dangerous. Wally aimed his weapon toward the trench and fired a burst of bullets. The Spanish riflemen were silenced. Then, together, Wally and Ayers carried Major Bell out of the line of fire.

Everyone who witnessed the performance of the black soldiers at Las Guasimas was impressed. Theodore Roosevelt, who later became president of the United States, led a group of soldiers known as the Rough Riders during the Spanish-American War. Commented Roosevelt, "I don't think that any Rough Rider will ever forget the tie that binds us to the Ninth and Tenth Cavalry."

Chapter 5

World War I

Henry Johnson

The soldiers of World War I fought from long trenches dug into the battlefields of Europe—the Americans and their allies on one side, the Germans on the other. An area known as "no man's land" stretched between the two forces, open and dangerous to enter.

Private Henry Johnson of the 369th Infantry stood on sentry duty on a May night in 1918. He and another soldier, Private Needham Roberts, guarded frontline trenches where French and American soldiers crouched against the earthen walls, trying to sleep.

The war had taken Johnson a long way from his birthplace, Albany, New York, and the town where his unit trained, Spartansburg, South Carolina. He was married and working as a redcap at Grand Central Station in New York City when the war began. He was one of the 367,000 African Americans who were called upon to serve in World War I.

At the training camp in South Carolina, Johnson and the other black New Yorkers met with resentment from the local whites. They were northerners who failed to understand the behavior expected of African Americans in the South. Too often, activities considered normal in the North got them into trouble. One black soldier stirred up hostile feelings simply by buying a newspaper at a hotel!

The army quickly sent the 369th Infantry overseas, before a serious confrontation could take place. Assigned to serve alongside a French unit, the 369th became the first black regiment to fight in Europe. They spent 191 days in the trenches—more than any other Americans.

Black soldiers performed a variety of duties in World War I. They served in the engineering corps, the signal corps, and the medical corps. There were black ambulance drivers, chaplains, surveyors, and draftsmen. Many African Americans belonged to labor battalions—driving trucks, unloading ships, digging trenches—although they were qualified to do much more.

Opportunities were better in the army, however, than in the other branches of the service. The marines accepted no African Americans at all. The navy permitted blacks to hold only low-level jobs.

Many young black men demanded the right to serve as officers in World War I. Students on the campuses of black colleges held demonstrations to protest inequality in the military.

At last the army gave in to the African Americans' demands. Six hundred thirty-nine black men were commissioned as army officers in October 1917. More became officers in the months that followed. They served with black regiments on the battlefields of Europe, regiments such as Henry Johnson's 369th Infantry.

The hours tended to pass slowly for the men on guard duty. It was well past midnight when Henry Johnson heard a rustle in the darkness. Suddenly, he and Needham Roberts heard gunfire. Some Germans had launched a surprise attack.

Although both men were wounded, Johnson shot back at the approaching enemy while Roberts threw grenades. But the Germans kept coming forward, moving in to capture the two guards. Johnson pulled a bolo knife from his belt—a short, heavy weapon that was razor sharp. He fought against several enemy soldiers hand to hand.

Then Johnson saw Roberts, now badly injured, in the arms of some Germans who were carrying him away. Johnson rushed forward and slashed at the Germans with his knife. He saved his fellow soldier from becoming a prisoner of war. Before

"Your record has sent a thrill of joy and satisfaction to the hearts of millions of black and white Americans, rich and poor, high and low."

the fight was over, Johnson killed at least four Germans and wounded eight more. He forced the surviving Germans to retreat.

The extraordinary heroism of one American soldier on that night in May 1918 has been called the "Battle of Henry Johnson."

Henry Johnson and Needham Roberts were the first Americans of any race to receive the *croix de guerre*, a French military decoration awarded for bravery. The American commander wrote to Johnson's wife, praising her husband's actions. "The Germans, doubtless thinking it was a host instead of two brave Colored boys fighting like tigers in a bay," he stated, "picked up their dead and wounded and slunk away."

In December 1918, Dr. Robert Moton, president of Tuskegee Institute, a college for African Americans, visited the black troops in Europe. "You have been tremendously tested," Moton told them. "Your record has sent a thrill of joy and satisfaction to the hearts of millions of black and white Americans, rich and poor, high and low." Moton promised the soldiers that they would return to America as heroes.

Henry Johnson spent months in the hospital waiting for his wounds to heal. He and the other soldiers of the 369th Infantry returned to the United States in February 1919. The war had ended in a victory for the Americans and their allies. As they paraded the length of Fifth Avenue in New York City and the cheers of a million spectators reached their ears, the men of the 369th felt like heroes, just as Robert Moton had promised.

But the good feeling did not last. The "Red Summer" of 1919 proved to be a time of racial violence and turmoil. Race riots broke out in cities across the nation. With black soldiers home from the war and black families moving into urban areas, whites feared competition from African Americans for jobs and housing.

"Make way for Democracy!" proclaimed a black publication, the *Crisis*. "We saved it in France, and by the Great Jehovah, we will save it in the U.S.A., or know the reason why."

Freddie Stowers

Corporal Freddie Stowers never made it home from the war. He went to France with Company C of the 371st Infantry. Like Henry Johnson's regiment, the 371st was a black unit serving under black and white officers.

On September 28, 1918, Stowers's regiment was in the Champagne-Marne section of northeastern France. The Allied leaders had ordered an attack on a hill held by the Germans, a site called Hill 188. The commanders chose Company C to take the lead.

Well hidden in their trenches, German machine gunners fired nonstop at the approaching Americans. They killed or wounded many men and nearly halted the assault. Then Company C's squad leader, Freddie Stowers, took charge, and the course of the battle changed.

Heedless of personal danger, Stowers crawled along the ground toward a trench housing a group of machine gunners. As bullets streamed over his head, he urged his fellow soldiers to follow. Inch by inch they approached the machine gun nest. Heavy fighting broke out when the Americans reached the German trench, but Stowers and his men succeeded in destroying the site.

Then Stowers motioned toward a second line of trenches. He shouted to the others to continue their attack. Bullets from the machine guns struck Stowers's body as he moved forward, wounding him severely. Stowers crawled ahead, encouraging his comrades to keep fighting, until he died.

The taking of Hill 188 was part of a larger plan to capture key territories held by the Germans. The 371st Infantry went on to take prisoners and seize valuable weapons and supplies from the enemy. Its members received many honors during

World War I. The Distinguished Service Cross went to ten black officers and twelve enlisted men of the 371st. Thirty-four black officers and eighty-nine enlisted men were awarded the *croix de guerre*.

For years, Freddie Stowers's heroism in World War I went unrecognized. In 1988, the Army began an investigation to find out why no African Americans had won the Medal of Honor for service in that war. Were there no black soldiers who deserved the medal, Army officials asked, or had the accomplishments of African Americans been overlooked?

Two years of study followed, as government researchers sifted through the many pages of military records in the National Archives, the building that stores federal documents in Washington, D.C. They discovered that Stowers's superiors had recommended him for the Medal of Honor, but that the army had never processed that recommendation.

Wishing to correct a seventy-year-old mistake, army leaders reviewed the events of September 28, 1918, to determine whether Stowers did indeed deserve his nation's highest military honor. The army chief of staff, the secretary of the army, the secretary of defense, and the chairman of the Joint Chiefs of Staff all told President George Bush that Stowers had earned the medal.

Freddie Stowers's sisters were at the White

President Bush awarded the Medal of Honor posthumously to Freddie Stowers. His sister, Mary Bowers, accepted the award.

House on April 24, 1991, to receive the Medal of Honor in his place. Stowers had set "such a courageous example of personal bravery and leadership that he inspired his men to follow him into the fray," stated the citation that accompanied the medal. "Inspired by Stowers's selfless heroism and bravery, Company C continued its attack against incredible odds, contributing to the capture of Hill 188 and causing heavy enemy casualties."

Chapter 6

World War II

Benjamin Davis, Sr.

Whenever the Ku Klux Klan marched in the South, most black people stayed indoors. The white racist organization had grown considerably since the 1919 riots. Its members had lynched, or executed without trial, seventy African Americans in the year following World War I.

Colonel Benjamin Davis was one African American who refused to be frightened by the Klan. In the early 1920s, he was teaching military science and tactics at the Tuskegee Institute in Alabama when the Klan announced it would march past the school. In full uniform, Davis watched the nighttime march from his brightly lit porch. His wife and three children—Olive, Benjamin, Jr., and Elnora—stood by his side. Through his example, Davis taught the children to respect themselves and their race.

Davis's belief in his own worth had taken him far. Born in 1877, he had decided to be a soldier as a child in Washington, D.C., after watching the cavalry on parade at Fort Myer, across the Potomac River in Virginia.

Benjamin Davis spent one year at Howard University, a historic black college in the nation's capital. At the outbreak of the Spanish-American War, he left school and joined the army as a first lieutenant. Several units of black soldiers with black officers were formed hastily in 1898, to meet the demands of war. The war ended before Davis had a chance to fight, and he was discharged from the armed forces.

Army life had appealed to Davis, though, and he tried to get an appointment to the United States Military Academy at West Point. When President William McKinley refused to appoint a black cadet, Davis enlisted in the army as a private, a soldier with the lowest army rank. In 1899, Benjamin Davis went west to join the 9th Cavalry.

At Fort Duchesne, Utah, Davis met Major Charles Young, the only black officer in the army at that time. Young took a liking to Private Davis and urged him to take a test to qualify as an officer. Davis studied for two years with Major Young's help, mastering technical points in history, geography, surveying, and drill regulations. He passed the test and was commissioned as a second lieutenant.

The new president, Theodore Roosevelt, signed

Davis's commissioning order. When an aide told Roosevelt that Davis was black, the president replied, "Bully for him. Only one thing counts—he has qualified for the place."

Davis married Elnora Dickerson, a Washington seamstress, in 1902. Elnora died in 1916, just days after the birth of her third child. In 1919, Davis married Sadie Overton, a professor of English at Wilberforce University. This marriage would last forty-seven years, until Sadie's death in 1966.

Davis was an officer who wanted to lead troops. The army, however, took great pains to keep the black officer from commanding white soldiers. Davis served with black forces in the Philippines in 1901. The United States had acquired these Southeast Asian islands from Spain following the Spanish-American War. In 1912, Davis was military attaché to Liberia. It was his job to advise the American ambassador on military matters. Between 1915 and 1917, Davis patrolled the Mexican border.

But most of his assignments were to teach military courses or to oversee black National Guard units in the United States. He spent the years of World War I not in Europe but back in the Philippines. Still, Benjamin Davis, Sr., served his country without complaining. He did the best job he could, wherever the army sent him. He rose in rank over the years, to captain and then to major.

"Only one thing counts—he has qualified for the place."

In 1929, Davis escorted the widows and mothers of men killed in World War I to Europe, to view their loved ones' graves. The sensitivity with which he carried out this assignment impressed his superiors, and Davis was promoted to the rank of colonel.

By the 1930s, trouble was brewing in Europe again. Germany's Nazi government, led by Adolf Hitler, sent occupying armies into Austria, Czechoslovakia, and Poland. The Nazis considered themselves members of a "master race." They promoted hatred of Jews and other minority groups. England and France declared war on Germany in 1939. In the Far East, Japan was seeking to enlarge its empire. Japanese forces invaded China in 1931 and again in 1937.

Once more, the United States maintained a neutral stance. But President Franklin Roosevelt saw the need to be cautious and prepare for war. The military began a peacetime draft, calling men into the service. The army also made history. On October 25, 1940, Benjamin Davis, Sr., received another promotion. He became the nation's first African-American general.

The United States entered World War II in December 1941, following a Japanese attack on the U.S. naval base at Pearl Harbor, Hawaii. Three days later, Germany and its ally, Italy, declared war on the United States.

Approximately one million African Americans served in the armed forces during World War II. Their own experiences with prejudice made them especially aware of the dangers of Nazi racism. As in wars past, blacks belonged to segregated army units, often commanded by white officers. However, African Americans made important gains during World War II. The Marine Corps ended a 167-year ban and enlisted black marines. The Coast Guard, too, opened its ranks to blacks. For the first time, black battalions operated tanks. Black women joined the Women's Army Corps and the Army Nurse Corps. A small number of black women joined the WAVES, the women's division of the navy.

With his many years of army experience, General Benjamin Davis was a valued adviser to the commanders in Europe. He later served as a special assistant to the secretary of the army.

In October 1942, Davis reported for duty in Great Britain. The army had asked him to investigate reports of friction between black and white soldiers.

Davis talked with the enlisted men and discovered that the African-American soldiers felt welcome in England. The English people lacked the prejudice so common in the United States. They looked upon the black soldiers simply as

Americans. Any discord between white and black Americans, Davis reported, resulted from "resentment on the part of the white troops against the way the British people entertained Negro troops." Davis concluded, "I fear overmuch emphasis is being placed on color in our Army."

General Davis went to Ramitelli, Italy, in September 1944. There he pinned a Distinguished Flying Cross to the chest of his son, Colonel Benjamin Davis, Jr. The younger Davis,

General Benjamin O. Davis, Sr., inspects troops in World War II

a graduate of West Point, commanded the first African-American fighter pilots. Known as the Tuskegee Airmen because they trained at Tuskegee Army Air Field, these men earned 800 medals for heroism in World War II. They received praise for shooting down German planes at Anzio, Italy, and elsewhere, helping to win important battles. On many bombing missions, their swift fighter planes protected the large bombers from enemy attack.

The war ended in a victory for the Americans and their allies in 1945. Three years later, with the world at peace, Davis retired from the military. That same year President Harry S Truman signed Executive Order 9981, ending segregation in the armed forces.

Davis continued to serve his country in retirement. In 1948, he represented the president of the United States in Liberia, on the 100th anniversary of that country's independence. As a member of the Battle Monuments Commission, he inspected the American cemeteries at Anzio and other World War II battle sites, to see that fallen soldiers had been properly honored.

General Benjamin Davis, Sr., American patriot and soldier, died in 1970, at age ninety-three. He was buried in Arlington National Cemetery, near Fort Myer, where he had watched the cavalry perform drills as a boy.

Dorie Miller

The ships of the U.S. Pacific fleet were docked and quiet as the sun rose over Pearl Harbor, Hawaii. It was a Sunday morning, December 7, 1941.

At first the Japanese planes appeared as specks in the brightening sky. They arrived quickly and without warning to begin their surprise attack.

As bombs and bullets fell from the air, the ships' crew members left their breakfasts and hurried to their battle stations. Messman First Class Dorie Miller of the battleship *West Virginia* was on deck at the time of the attack. He was carrying laundry—napkins and tablecloths for the ship's dining room. Miller, a native of Waco, Texas, had joined the navy after leaving high school. Like all African Americans in the navy at that time, he worked in the kitchen.

A bomb struck the *West Virginia* and exploded. The force of the blast knocked Miller down. Shaken but unhurt, he got to his feet and looked around. Smoke from explosions and fires filled the air, and the Japanese planes kept coming. Then Miller saw the captain of the ship lying on the deck, badly injured and bleeding heavily.

A muscular man who had recently won a boxing contest, Miller carried his commander to a spot protected by a bulkhead, or partition. There, a medical corpsman could attend to the captain with some safety. Then Miller looked for a way to help defend his ship.

He saw that no one was firing one of the machine guns fastened to the deck. He had never been trained to use it. In fact, messmen were not permitted to fire weapons. But this was a time for fast thinking, not regulations. The country was under attack.

As the *West Virginia* started to sink, sea water crept across the deck. Dorie Miller figured out how to operate the powerful gun. Then he took aim at the planes overhead and fired. He kept on shooting until he ran out of ammunition. He destroyed at least four—and possibly six—of the attacking planes. Just before the *West Virginia* slipped below the surface of the harbor, Miller and the other surviving crew members abandoned ship.

For two hours, Japanese bombers and fighter planes attacked from the sky while Japanese submarines fired torpedoes that moved swiftly and silently toward the ships.

The assault that drew the United States into World War II devastated the Pacific fleet. Eighteen ships, including the *West Virginia*, were sunk or badly damaged. The raid destroyed nearly 200 planes on military airfields nearby. Three hundred Americans were killed or wounded.

Some early reports of the attack identified Dorie Miller merely as "a Negro cook who fired at Japanese planes." African Americans protested those accounts, which played down Miller's achievements. Miller should be commended, they said, for aiding the wounded captain and shooting down four planes.

The outcry brought Miller's actions to the attention of the Navy's leaders. On June 10, 1942, Admiral Chester W. Nimitz, commander in chief of the Pacific fleet, presented the twenty-one-year-old seaman with the Navy Cross, the navy's highest award for bravery. The navy honored Miller "for his distinguished devotion to duty, extraordinary courage and disregard for his own personal safety."

People throughout the United States learned about Dorie Miller, the first American hero of World War II. Miller appeared at bond drives, rallies where people were urged to buy savings bonds to support the war.

Miller's heroism led to new opportunities in the navy for African Americans. One month after the United States entered the war, President Franklin Roosevelt ordered the navy to change its racial policy and allow black sailors to perform all duties aboard ship. The navy also trained African Americans to be officers. Fifty-two black naval officers served in World War II.

Dorie Miller, wearing the Navy Cross

On Thanksgiving Day, 1943, Miller was serving aboard an aircraft carrier, the U.S.S. *Liscombe Bay*, in the South Pacific. A torpedo from a Japanese submarine tore into the side of the ship and sank it. More than 600 crew members died, among them Dorie Miller.

Ruben Rivers

D-Day. June 6, 1944. On this date, American and British forces landed at Normandy, on the northern coast of France. They began a long, tough push into Europe, to free France and other countries from German occupation. The armies planned to move forward toward Germany and victory in Europe.

On June 9, three days after the Normandy invasion, the 761st Tank Battalion was ordered overseas. This unit of black fighting men had waited a long time to enter the war. Many of the soldiers had been training at army bases since April 1942. They had remained in the United States while white tank battalions served in the war. Most of the army's leaders doubted that blacks could handle the heavy armored vehicles.

The soldiers of the 761st arrived in France on October 10. Among them was Sergeant Ruben Rivers of Tecumseh, Oklahoma. Born in 1921, Rivers was one of twelve brothers and sisters. Now he was one of 750 black tankers serving under General George S. Patton, one of the toughest commanders in the army.

Patton had requested the 761st for his push toward Paris. He had confidence in their courage and skill. "I don't care what color you are," Patton told the men. "I would never have asked for you if you weren't good. I have nothing but the best in my Army."

Patton reminded the black soldiers that African Americans in the United States would be following the news of their achievements. "Your race is looking forward to you. Don't let them down," he said. "Don't let me down."

On November 7, Rivers's company was leading a column of infantrymen, or foot soldiers, when they came upon a roadblock that had been put in place by the Germans. German soldiers fired guns at the stalled American column, but that didn't stop Ruben Rivers from climbing out of his tank. He attached a cable to the roadblock and hauled it out of the way. He enabled the army to continue its mission. Rivers's courage and quick thinking earned him the Silver Star, awarded for gallantry in action.

The 761st went into battle the next day at 6 AM, at the front of Patton's attacking force. True to their motto, "Come Out Fighting," they broke through enemy defenses and protected the infantry that followed.

On November 18, 1944, Patton's troops captured the French town of Guebling from the Germans after several days of battle. The fight for the town was fierce. A hunk of shrapnel—a flying piece

"I don't care what color you are. I would never have asked for you if you weren't good. I have nothing but the best in my Army."

of metal—hit Rivers's leg and tore it open to the bone. Rivers's commander, David Williams, ordered the wounded soldier to be evacuated for treatment and then sent home. "Hey, this is your chance," Williams told Rivers. "Your war is over."

But Rivers ignored the order. He turned down a shot of morphine to kill his pain. "You need me," he said. Ruben Rivers fought on until November 19, when he died in an assault on German gun positions.

During 183 straight days of combat, the 761st Tank Battalion proved to be a potent fighting force. They seized more than thirty towns, took 15,800 prisoners, and killed six thousand enemy soldiers. According to some reports, members of the battalion helped free Jewish survivors from Nazi concentration camps. The Nazis murdered millions of people, including six million Jews, in those camps of death.

The men of the 761st earned many decorations during World War II, including 11 Silver Stars, 69 Bronze Stars, and 296 Purple Hearts, which are awarded to soldiers wounded in battle. But it wasn't until 1978 that the battalion was honored with a Presidential Unit Citation, "for extraordinary heroism in military operations against an armed enemy."

No one from the black tank unit received the

Medal of Honor. In fact, not one of the 470 Medals of Honor awarded for service in World War II went to an African American.

Today, many Americans contend that the government has ignored the contributions of blacks during that war. Some are trying to change that situation. David Williams has been working on behalf of Ruben Rivers, the soldier he commanded fifty years ago. Williams and Rivers's sister, Anese Rivers Woodfork, have brought Ruben's case to the attention of the federal government. They want to obtain the Medal of Honor for him, although 1952, the deadline for such awards, is long past.

Williams and Woodfork are hopeful the government will waive the deadline for Ruben Rivers as it did for Freddie Stowers, the Medal of Honor winner from World War I. According to David Williams, Rivers deserves the medal for a very simple reason. "Nobody surpassed his feat," he said.

Chapter 7
The Korean War

William Thompson

Life was hard for William Thompson. He was born into poverty in Brooklyn, New York, and there were times when his mother could not care for him. A minister discovered young William sleeping in a city park one night and took him to a shelter for homeless boys. There William slept under a roof each night. He ate three meals a day and attended school. The shelter was William's home until 1945, when he was eighteen years old and was drafted into the army.

Thompson served as a soldier for one and one-half years. He returned to New York in February 1947 but soon grew unhappy with civilian life. He missed the routine of the military. During his brief time in the service, the army had begun to feel like home. In June 1948, he reenlisted.

William Thompson came back to an army that was changing. Just four months earlier, President Truman had ended segregation in the armed forces. Truman hoped to uphold "the highest standards of democracy" in the U.S. military.

Black and white soldiers were just starting to serve together in integrated units when war broke out again. On June 25, 1950, communist North Korea invaded its neighbor, South Korea. China and the Soviet Union were providing North Korea with equipment and soldiers.

Troops from the United States traveled to Asia as part of a multinational effort to help South Korea fight off the invasion. Private William Thompson went to Korea as a member of Company M, 24th Infantry Regiment.

On the night of August 6, 1950, Thompson's platoon was near Haman, South Korea, organizing their equipment and making plans. They felt protected by the darkness, but safety was only an illusion. Without warning, a large enemy force attacked the men of Company M.

Things looked bad for the Americans. They were outnumbered and fighting on strange, mountainous terrain. If William Thompson felt fear, however, he kept it to himself. He set up his machine gun in the path of the oncoming North Korean and Chinese soldiers and sprayed the attackers with bullets. He shot steadily and accurately, giving his comrades a chance to reach a safer position.

Enemy bullets and fragments of exploding grenades struck Thompson's body. His fellow soldiers begged him to retreat. They worried that he would be killed. "Maybe I won't get out," Thompson shouted back, "but I'm going to take a lot of them with me." Then he let loose another blast of machine gun fire. As Thompson's friends feared, his one-man defense ended when a North Korean grenade took his life.

In recognition of his outstanding action, Private William Thompson was honored with the Medal of Honor after his death. Thompson was the first African American to be awarded the Medal of Honor in the twentieth century. He was one of only two black soldiers from the Korean War to be so honored. The other black Medal of Honor winner, Sergeant Cornelius Charlton, gave his life while leading an attack on an enemy position.

On June 21, 1951, Thompson's mother, Mary Henderson, traveled to the Pentagon, the headquarters of the Defense Department, near Washington, D.C. There she received her son's medal from General Omar N. Bradley, chairman of the Joint Chiefs of Staff. One of the general's aides read the citation that accompanied the medal. "Private Thompson's dauntless courage and self-sacrifice," noted the aide, "reflect the highest credit on himself and uphold the esteemed tradition of military service."

Chapter 8

The Vietnam War

Lawrence Joel

Specialist Lawrence Joel's army career took him to places throughout the world. Born and raised in Winston-Salem, North Carolina, Joel enlisted in the army in 1946. He served in Germany, in Italy, and on the Japanese island of Okinawa. He was a medical aidman, trained to give emergency treatment to injured soldiers. In 1965, Joel went to Southeast Asia, to a hot, steamy country called Vietnam.

Between 1965 and 1973, American combat forces fought in the long conflict known as the Vietnam War. Once a single nation, Vietnam had separated into two countries in 1954. Now the Vietcong, communist forces from North Vietnam, were fighting to overthrow the democratic government of South Vietnam. The South Vietnamese had asked the United States for help.

The war in Vietnam divided the American people. Many opposed American involvement, claiming U.S. troops did not belong in another nation's civil war. They voiced concerns that the United States could never win a jungle war so far from home. The Reverend Martin Luther King, Jr., and other African Americans said the war cost money that could be better spent to battle racism and poverty at home.

Many other Americans, both black and white, supported the American war effort. Among them was Specialist Lawrence Joel.

On November 6, 1965, the soldiers of Joel's unit, men of the 503rd Infantry, suddenly found themselves under attack by a large number of Vietcong who were hidden well in the lush jungle growth. The first gunfire wiped out the advance squad of Joel's company, killing or wounding nearly every man.

As the rest of the soldiers pressed forward into battle, Joel stayed behind and treated the wounded. Then, because more soldiers had been hit, he hurried ahead to the site of the fighting.

Crouching to avoid the flying bullets that seemed to be everywhere, Specialist Joel moved from one wounded soldier to another. He bandaged torn limbs and injected suffering soldiers with medication to deaden their pain. He held up bags of plasma that dripped into the veins of those who had bled heavily.

He saved one soldier's life by placing a plastic

bag over a gaping chest wound. The bag slowed the man's bleeding and allowed his blood to congeal. This was not a technique Joel had been taught. He simply did the best that he could with whatever was at hand.

At thirty-eight, Joel was twice as old as some of the men he treated. Among the wounded and dying men were soldiers not much older than his own children, Cornelius, fourteen, and Deborah, twelve. He treated a number of African Americans.

Black personnel made up a large percentage of the American fighting force in the war. At the end of 1965, more than 20,000 African Americans were in Vietnam. By 1972, they made up 17 percent of the American presence. Black soldiers were more likely than whites to be in combat roles—and to be wounded or killed. They accounted for more than one-fifth of the combat deaths in 1966.

There were still wounded men needing help when a bullet ripped into Lawrence Joel's leg. He paused in his work to clean and dress his wound. He gave himself a shot of morphine, a drug to ease the pain. Then he resumed his task of saving lives. He often had to crawl through a storm of bullets to reach an injured soldier.

The battle slackened after twenty-four exhausting hours. Four hundred Vietcong were dead. Now enemy snipers concealed in the plant growth aimed

their rifles at the American soldiers. They tried to pick off the Americans one by one. Weary and in pain, Joel treated his fellow soldiers until his commander ordered him flown to a hospital. His work was done. He had saved many lives and had set an example of courage and devotion for all who saw him.

Specialist Lawrence Joel stood at the White House on March 9, 1967, with his wife, Dorothy, and his children. He received the Medal of Honor from President Lyndon Johnson. He was one of twenty black Medal of Honor winners from the Vietnam War. Johnson praised Joel's bravery and devotion to others. "As we salute the valor of this soldier," Johnson said, "we salute the best in the American tradition."

Lawrence Joel and his wife stand on either side of President Johnson at the White House ceremony when Joel received the Medal of Honor

Fred V. Cherry

As a child, Fred Cherry often paused on his long walk to school to watch military planes fly overhead. Pilots were training for service in World War II at a naval base near Fred's home in rural Suffolk, Virginia. If the planes flew low enough, the boy waved to the pilots inside.

At home, Fred read newspaper articles about the Tuskegee Airmen and the battles they had won.

Fred admired these brave pilots who were African Americans like himself. "I'm going to be a fighter pilot just as soon as I get old enough," he vowed.

But for a while Fred's life took another course. When he was eleven years old, his father died. Money was tight for his mother and her large family, so Fred went to live with his married sister, Beulah.

Beulah saw that Fred had intelligence. She encouraged him to work hard in school and make something of himself. She urged him to become a doctor. Fred finished high school and entered college with the goal of studying biology. A degree in biology, the science of life, would prepare him for medical school. Fred plugged away at his studies, but without joy. "What I really wanted to do was fly planes," he said.

Just before he graduated from college, Fred Cherry went to Langley Air Force Base in Norfolk, Virginia. There he took the written and physical tests to enter flight school. Twenty young men took the series of tests. Cherry was the only African American in the group, and he earned the highest score.

Fred Cherry entered the air force in October 1951. When he completed flight school, the air force sent him to Korea. He flew more than fifty missions in the Korean War.

In the 1960s, Fred Cherry had a wife and four children and was stationed in Japan. He had to leave his family behind when he went to Thailand. He was stationed there for two months to fly bombing missions over North Vietnam. His bombs destroyed enemy military targets, bridges, and roads.

On October 25, 1965, Cherry was leading a squadron of planes over enemy territory. He had one more week to serve in Thailand before going home. The group was three minutes away from its target when Cherry heard a "thump." His plane had been hit by gunfire, but it could still fly. He flew to his target, dropped his bombs, and turned around. Then Cherry saw smoke coming from his instrument panel. Just moments later, the plane blew up.

Cherry ejected safely from the craft and hit the ground hard. He looked around and saw he was surrounded by Vietcong soldiers. He tried to raise his hands but could only raise one. His left shoulder and wrist had broken when he fell. When he stood up to walk, he found that his ankle was broken, too.

The Vietcong brought Cherry to Hoa Lo Prison, a place the American prisoners called the "Hanoi Hilton." He was the forty-third American and the first black to be captured in North

Vietnam. The Vietcong tortured Cherry and kept him in a rat-infested cell. They questioned him about his mission and his plane. As he had been instructed, Cherry told them only his name, rank, serial number, and date of birth.

On November 16, his captors moved Fred Cherry to Cu Loc Prison, nicknamed "the Zoo." There he shared a cell with another prisoner. Porter Halyburton, known as "Hally," was a white man from the South. The two distrusted each other at first but in time became friends. They helped each other survive.

Slowly, Cherry's wrist and ankle healed, but his shoulder remained injured. North Vietnamese doctors operated on him in February 1966 and covered his upper body in a large cast. Beneath the cast, Cherry's shoulder grew badly infected. He developed a high fever. He became so ill that he lost touch with reality. He sometimes thought he was flying missions or eating in a restaurant.

Hally fed his suffering cellmate and tried to keep his wound clean. Still, when the doctors removed the cast a month after the operation, Cherry was barely alive. His weight had dropped to eighty pounds.

Fred Cherry had another operation, this time without any anesthesia to block the pain of surgery. The doctors kept watching his face for signs of

Fred Cherry

65

distress, but Cherry refused to give them satisfaction. "Each time they looked down at me," he said, "I would look at them and smile."

Worse than the pain of surgery, though, was the loss of a friend. Four days after returning Cherry to his cell, the Vietcong moved Hally to new quarters. The two friends would not meet again until after the war.

Cherry and the other prisoners often suffered beatings with rubber strips and bamboo sticks. They spent many days in solitary confinement. Cherry once endured fifty-three straight weeks alone in a cell.

A few prisoners gave information to their captors in exchange for better treatment. Cherry refused to do this. The North Vietnamese asked Cherry why he remained loyal to the United States when African Americans were treated unequally there. "A soldier's a soldier," Cherry replied. "I'm still an officer in the United States services. I will respect that, and I would hope that you will respect that of me." Through all of the torture and questioning, Cherry thought about the twenty-four million black Americans he represented. "I'm just not going to denounce my government or shame my people," he stated.

In January 1973, the United States and North Vietnam reached an agreement that provided for the release of prisoners of war. Fred Cherry was freed. He was flown to the Philippines, where he enjoyed his first good meal in seven years. Then he came home to the United States, where army doctors examined his shoulder. The doctors told Cherry it would never move normally again.

The years of Cherry's imprisonment had been hard for his family as well. His mother had died. He and his wife had grown apart, and they later divorced. Cherry was especially sorry to learn that his two sons had dropped out of school.

The government honored Fred Cherry with the Air Force Cross and two Bronze Stars for heroism, and two Purple Hearts for being wounded in combat. He had already earned the Distinguished Flying Cross and the Silver Star. In 1981, Colonel Cherry retired from the air force after thirty years of service.

Fred Cherry settled in Silver Spring, Maryland, near Washington, D.C. He married again and started a business, Cherry Engineering Support Services. This company supervises the design and development of complex equipment for air traffic control and other flight-related fields.

The former prisoner of war often speaks to young people about his experiences. He urges them to get a good education. He tells children, "You must set your goals high. If you set them low, you are going to end up low."

When he thinks back on his years in prison, Fred Cherry feels no regret. "Hadn't I done that, my life would have been totally different," he said. "I might not be here today."

Chapter 9

The Persian Gulf War

Lonnie Davis

Sergeant First Class Lonnie Davis's favorite subject is his family. Of the eighteen children in the Davis family, ten have served their country in the army, the navy, or the marines. Their combined service equals more than ninety years. "So as you can see, we have a long and proud military heritage," Sergeant Davis said.

Lonnie Davis was born in rural Georgia in 1958. "I was a weird child," he said. "I didn't like sports." Lonnie enjoyed science, and he read many books. He liked to read about far-off places in the encyclopedia. "I was fascinated by learning different things," he added.

When he was small, Lonnie took long walks with one of his older brothers, Andrew. Andrew told him the names of plants and animals and taught him to love nature. On one of those walks,

Andrew told five-year-old Lonnie that he was going away. He had enlisted in the marines. Like their brother James, who was in the navy, Andrew felt an obligation to serve his country. If necessary, he would fight to defend the American way of life.

Although he was young, Lonnie understood Andrew's reasons for enlisting. "My parents stressed three things to us when we were growing up," he explained. "Get a good education. Do not use drugs or in any other way abuse our bodies. Always keep faith in God and country."

Lonnie felt confused, he said, when Andrew was killed in Vietnam in 1967. He missed his brother; at the same time, he was proud of what Andrew had done. As Lonnie grew older, he saw two more of his brothers enter the armed forces. Charles Davis joined the army in 1969, and Johnnie Davis soon enlisted in the army as well.

Military service attracted Lonnie when he finished high school in 1976, and five more Davis brothers would follow in his footsteps. Every young person in the small town of Masella, Georgia, seemed to be competing for the same few jobs. The army offered Lonnie the chance for a career. It also gave him the opportunity to see some of the places he had read about.

Lonnie Davis has been stationed at sites as distant as South Korea and Alaska. While stationed in Germany, he visited Berlin, a city then divided by a thick, impenetrable wall. Residents were forbidden to pass from one side of the city to the other. More than ever, he appreciated the freedom guaranteed to Americans by the Constitution. He felt grateful for the opportunity to serve his country.

On December 23, 1990, Sergeant Lonnie Davis left a military base in Germany for the deserts of the Middle East. Saddam Hussein, ruler of Iraq, had sent an invading force into the nation of Kuwait. With Kuwait quickly captured, the Iraqi army moved to the border of another Persian Gulf nation, Saudi Arabia.

The United Nations imposed economic sanctions against Iraq soon after the invasion. U.N. member nations agreed not to sell goods to Iraq until Saddam Hussein's army retreated. The Iraqis ignored the sanctions, though, and remained in Kuwait. Now President George Bush was ready to take action. He sent American forces—467,000 men and women—to the Middle East. One of those soldiers was Lonnie Davis.

Davis expected the desert to be hot, and there were days when the temperature reached 120 degrees Fahrenheit. He never expected cold and rain. But he soon learned that severe rainstorms did occur in Saudi Arabia. Sometimes, on the changeable desert, the soldiers could see for miles. Later, during sandstorms, they could barely see things five feet away. Blowing sand made it hard to breathe.

President Bush ordered the American forces to attack the Iraqis. The assault known as Operation Desert Storm began on January 17, 1991. Lonnie Davis's task force set to work. Their job was precision firing, shooting at targets up to twenty-six miles away. Sergeant Davis monitored the operation. He made sure the gunmen received accurate information about the location of their targets. He saw to it that his task force struck no friendly forces by mistake.

Thirty-eight days after the attack began, the Americans moved across the border into Kuwait. Lonnie Davis rode in an army vehicle beside a soldier who had just turned eighteen. For the first time, the precision firing unit witnessed the destruction of war at close range. Bodies were everywhere. Davis noted that the eighteen-year-old, upon seeing so much death, seemed to grow older before his eyes.

President Bush called for a cease-fire four days later. The war had been won. Kuwait was an independent nation again.

Davis carried home vivid memories when he left the Middle East in May 1991. He recalled the way thousands of Iraqi soldiers, men who

Lonnie Davis

had been forced to fight, surrendered willingly to the Americans.

The sight of an armored fighting vehicle with an American flag on its antenna remained in Davis's memory. He felt pride in his country, he said, when an A-10 aircraft flying past the vehicle dipped its wing in a salute. Davis would often remember giving food and supplies to the Iraqi people after the war ended.

Sergeant First Class Lonnie Davis was one of 113,000 African Americans who fought in the Persian Gulf War. Today, he continues his army career, carrying on his family's tradition of service. As he likes to say, "I'm going to keep on doing the job that I am doing as long as I can do it!"

Conclusion

From the time of Crispus Attucks and the first stirrings of revolt in the thirteen English colonies, blacks have defended freedom for themselves and others. They fought for their nation even while it kept their race in slavery. From the streets of colonial Boston to the deserts of the Middle East, they proved themselves equal to white forces.

Black fighting men have fired rifles and driven tanks. They have used muscle power and brain power to win important battles. Whether piloting ships and planes, enduring torture, or leading troops in war, these Americans have made history.

Chronology:

African Americans in the U.S. Armed Forces

1770	On March 5, Crispus Attucks, a former slave, is among the first to die in the "Boston Massacre."
1776-1781	7,000 African-American soldiers and sailors take part in the Revolutionary War.
1776	On January 16, the Continental Congress agrees to enlist free blacks.
1812-1815	Black soldiers and sailors fight against the British troops at such critical battles as Lake Erie and New Orleans.
1862-1865	186,000 African-American soldiers serve in black regiments during the Civil War; 38,000 black soldiers lose their lives in more than 400 battles.
1862	On July 17, the U.S. Congress approves the enlistment of black soldiers.
1865	On March 13, the Confederate States of America begins to accept black recruits.
1866-1890	Units of black soldiers, referred to as Buffalo Soldiers, are formed as part of the U.S. Army.
1872	On September 21, John H. Conyers becomes the first African American admitted to the U.S. Naval Academy.
1877	On June 15, Henry O. Flipper becomes the first African American to graduate from West Point.
1914-1918	More than 400,000 African Americans serve in the U.S. armed forces during the First World War.

On May 15, two black soldiers, Henry Johnson and Needham Roberts become the first Americans to receive the French Medal of Honor (*croix de guerre*).	1918
In June, Benjamin O. Davis, Jr., graduates from West Point, the first black American to do so in the twentieth century.	1936
Benjamin O. Davis, Sr., becomes the first African-American general in the active Regular Army.	1940
American forces in World War II include more than a million African-American men and women.	1941-1945
On March 25, the Army Air Corps forms its first black unit, the 99th Pursuit Squadron.	1941
On August 24, Colonel Benjamin O. Davis, Jr., is made commander of the 99th Pursuit Squadron.	1942
On January 27 and 28, the airmen of the 99th Pursuit Squadron score a major victory against enemy fighters at the Italian seaside town of Anzio.	1944
On February 2, President Harry S Truman signs Executive Order 9981, ordering an end to segregation in the U.S. armed forces.	1948
Black and white forces fight side by side in Korea as separate black fighting units are disbanded.	1950-1953
Twenty African-American soldiers are awarded the Medal of Honor during the Vietnam War.	1965-1973
On April 28, Samuel L. Gravely becomes the first black admiral in the history of the U.S. Navy.	1971
In August, Daniel "Chappie" James becomes the first African American to achieve the rank of four-star general.	1975
On October 3, Colin Powell becomes the first African-American chairman of the Joint Chiefs of Staff.	1989
100,000 African-American men and women are sent to the Middle East during the Persian Gulf conflict.	1990-1991
On July 25, the Buffalo Soldier Monument is dedicated at Fort Leavenworth, Kansas.	1992

Index

References to photographs are listed in *italic, **boldface*** type.

Bibliography

Adams, Russell L. *Great Negroes Past and Present, Third Edition.* Chicago: Afro-Am Publishing Company, 1969.

Altman, Susan. *Extraordinary Black Americans from Colonial to Contemporary Times.* Chicago: Childrens Press, 1989.

Bernstein, Richard. "Comrades and Family Fighting to Honor a Hero." *New York Times,* March 28, 1993.

Franklin, John Hope. *From Slavery to Freedom: A History of Negro Americans, Fifth Edition.* New York: Alfred A. Knopf, 1980.

Greene, Robert Ewell. *Black Defenders of America: 1775-1973.* Chicago: Johnson Publishing Company, 1974.

Leckie, William H. *The Buffalo Soldiers: A Narrative of the Negro Cavalry in the West.* Norman, OK: University of Oklahoma Press, 1967.

Lee, Irvin H. *Negro Medal of Honor Men, Second Edition.* New York: Dodd, Mead & Company, 1967.

Mullen, Robert W. *Blacks in America's Wars: The Shift in Attitudes from the Revolutionary War to Vietnam.* New York: Monad Press, 1973.

Office of the Deputy Assistant Secretary of Defense for Civilian Personnel Policy/Equal Opportunity. *Black Americans in Defense of Our Nation.* Washington, D C: U.S. Government Printing Office, 1991.

Terry, Wallace, ed. *Bloods: An Oral History of the Vietnam War by Black Veterans.* New York: Ballantine Books, 1984.

Wakin, Edward. *Black Fighting Men in U.S. History.* New York: Lothrop, Lee & Shepard Co., 1971.